Jan 14/2013

Out of this World Jokes About the Solar System

Laugh and Learn About Science

Melissa Stewart

Illustrated by Gerald Kelley

Enslow Elementary, an imprint of Enslow Publishers, Inc.

Enslow Elementary is a registered trademark of Enslow Publishers, Inc.

Library of Congress Cataloging-in-Publication Data

Stewart, Melissa.

Out of this world jokes about the solar system : laugh and learn about science / Written by Melissa Stewart ; Illustrated by Gerald Kelley.

p. cm. — (Super silly science jokes)

Includes index.

Summary: "Learn about the planets in our solar system, the Kuiper Belt, asteroids, and more. Read jokes about all of these topics, and learn how to write your own"—Provided by publisher.

ISBN 978-0-7660-3970-4

1. Solar system—Miscellanea—Juvenile literature. 2. Wit and humor—Juvenile literature. I. Kelley, Gerald, ill. II. Title.

QB501.3.S74 2013

523.202'07—dc23

2011026529

Future editions:

Paperback ISBN 978-1-4644-0166-4

ePUB ISBN 978-1-4645-1073-1

PDF ISBN 978-1-4646-1073-8

Printed in China

012012 Leo Paper Group, Heshan City, Guangdong, China

10 9 8 7 6 5 4 3 2 1

To Our Readers: We have done our best to make sure all Internet Addresses in this book were active and appropriate when we went to press. However, the author and the publisher have no control over and assume no liability for the material available on those Internet sites or on other Web sites they may link to. Any comments or suggestions can be sent by e-mail to comments@enslow.com or to the address on the back cover.

Illustration Credits: © 2011 Gerald Kelley (www.geraldkelley.com)

Photo Credits: EAS–AOES Medialab, p. 19; ESA 2002, p. 32; Enslow Publishers, Inc., p. 44; European Space Agency, p. 15 (comet); Illustration by AOES Medialab, International Astronomical Union/Martin Kornmesser, p. 28; Lawrence Sromovsky, University of Wisconsin-Madison/W. M. Keck, p. 24; Lunar and Planetary Institute, p. 11; NASA, pp. 7, 27, 35, 36; NASA: Greg Shirah, pp. 3, 4, Johns Hopkins University Applied Physics Laboratory/Carnegie Institute, p. 8, JPL, pp. 16, 20, JPL/Space Science Institute, p. 23, JPL/USGS, p. 15 (asteroid), Visible Earth, p. 12; NASA and G. Bacon (Space Telescope Science Institute), p. 31; Shutterstock.com, pp. 1, 38, 41, 43.

Cover Illustration: © 2011 Gerald Kelley (www.geraldkelley.com)

Enslow Elementary

an imprint of

Enslow Publishers, Inc.
40 Industrial Road
Box 398
Berkeley Heights, NJ 07922
USA

http://www.enslow.com

Contents

1 Welcome to the Solar System

What's the **solar system**? It's our place in space.

The Sun is the star of our solar system. Its massive **gravity** pulls at eight planets, five dwarf planets, and millions of smaller objects. Most of these objects—planets, comets, asteroids, **meteoroids**—move in circles around the Sun. But a few **orbit** nearby planets. They are called **moons** and **rings**.

As you read this book, you'll learn all kinds of cool facts about our solar system. But that's not all. This book is also chock full of jokes. Some of them will make you laugh out loud. Others might make you groan. (Sorry.) But either way, you'll have a heck of a good time. So let's get started!

Q: What did the comet say to the Sun?

A: "You are very attractive."

Q: What happened when the Moon tried to run away from home?

A: He suddenly understood the gravity of his situation.

Fun With the Sun

The night sky twinkles with the light of billions of stars. But during the day, we only see one star—the Sun.

The Sun isn't the biggest star in the universe. But it looks gigantic to us. That's because it's so close.

What's the Sun made of? Burning gases. And boy, are they hot! The Sun's surface is a fiery 11,000 degrees Fahrenheit (6,000 degrees Celsius). Sizzlin'!

The Sun and the rest of the solar system formed about 4.5 billion years ago. Scientists think our star will keep on burning bright for another 5 million years. That's good news because life on Earth couldn't survive without the Sun's heat and light.

Q: Why doesn't the Sun go to college?

A: It already has thousands of degrees.

Q: What does the star of our solar system like to eat for dessert?

A: A hot fudge sun-dae.

Q: What did Earth say to the Sun?

A: You're the light of my life!

Mini Mercury

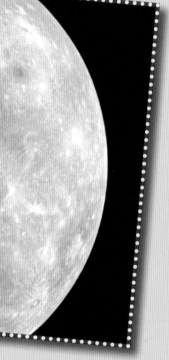

Mercury is the smallest planet in the solar system. And it just keeps getting smaller. Scientists think it has shrunk up to a mile (2 kilometers) since it formed.

Because Mercury is so small, it has very little gravitational pull. That means it can't hold on to much of an **atmosphere**—the layer of gases around a planet.

The surface of Mercury looks a lot like our Moon. Some areas are covered with **craters**. Other areas are smooth.

The little planet takes just eighty-eight Earth **days** to go around the Sun. That's the shortest **year** in the solar system. But a day on Mercury—the time it takes to spin once—is as long as two months on Earth. Wow!

Q: What did the Sun say to Mercury as the solar system formed?

A: "Won't you be my neighbor?"

GOOD EATS!

Q: Did you hear about the new restaurant on Mercury?

A: It has great food, but not much atmosphere.

4 Venus: It's Hot! Hot! Hot!

Because Mercury is the planet closest to the Sun, you might think that it is the hottest planet in the solar system. But think again. That honor goes to Venus.

Venus is farther from the Sun than Mercury. But its thick atmosphere traps the Sun's hot rays. That makes the planet's surface heat up to a sizzling 900°F (482°C). Yowzah!

The Sun may not be the only thing heating up Venus. More than 100,000 volcanoes dot the planet's surface. And scientists have spotted signs of recent lava flows.

Venus spins very slowly, so its days are really long—243 Earth days long. Because Venus is close to the Sun, its years are fairly short—just 228 Earth days. That means the days on Venus are longer than the years. Now that's incredible!

Q: What did Mercury say to Venus?

A: "You're hot stuff!"

Q: Why don't comets like to cruise past Venus?

A: They're afraid of Venus flytraps.

5 Home, Sweet Home

Some people call Earth the blue planet—and with good reason. More than 70 percent of our planet is covered with water. That's what makes Earth so special. Living things couldn't survive without all that water.

Like Venus, Earth has a thick atmosphere. And below our feet, the planet has four layers—the **crust**, the **mantle**, the outer **core**, and the inner core. The mantle contains hot, liquid rock called magma. The inner core and outer core are made of metals.

Earth has something that Venus and Mercury don't: a moon. It circles Earth once every twenty-seven days. That's just about a month. A day on Earth lasts twenty-four hours. And a year on our planet has 365 days.

Q: How is Earth like a piece of bread?

A: It has a crust.

Q: Why did Venus think Earth was sad?

A: Because it looked so blue.

What's a Shooting Star?

Have you ever seen a shooting star whiz across the night sky? It's a magical sight.

But that light isn't really coming from a star. It's coming from a meteoroid—a small piece of space rock. Many meteoroids are smaller than a pea. A few are as big as a boulder. Scientists call the streak of light a **meteor**.

Why do we see that bright glow? Because the chunk of rock burns up as it travels through Earth's atmosphere. Sometimes many meteors appear in just a few minutes. That's called a **meteor shower**.

Every day, bits of space rock land on Earth. They are called **meteorites**. But don't worry. Most of them are too small to do any damage.

asteroid

Q: Why did the asteroid eat a hot dog instead of mac and cheese?

A: Because a hot dog is meteor.

comet

Q: What did the comet do when the Sun told it to clean up its act?

A: It took a meteor shower.

7 Mysterious Mars

Mars has the tallest mountain in the solar system—and the deepest canyon. It also has the fiercest twisters. No wonder Mars has fascinated people for centuries.

Mars is about half the size of Earth. Deep channels crisscross the planet's rusty-red surface. Scientists think the channels may have carried water long, long ago.

Like Mercury, Mars has almost no atmosphere. But guess what Mars does have—two small moons. Phobos and Deimos orbit very close to their parent planet.

A day on Mars is about twenty-four hours long. But the red planet takes almost twice as long as Earth to orbit the Sun. Its year lasts 688 Earth days.

Q: How did Mars become the red planet?

A: It stayed out in the sun too long.

Q: What is Phobos's favorite snack?

A: A Mars bar.

Q: What did the alien say as his spaceship passed Mars?

A: Red alert! Red alert!

8 Watch Out for Asteroids!

What's an **asteroid**? It's a rocky object that's larger than a meteoroid but smaller than a planet. Sometimes asteroids crash and break into meteoroids.

Many asteroids are about one mile (two kilometers) across. But the largest one is 605 miles (974 kilometers) wide. That's about the distance from Boston, Massachusetts, to Raleigh, North Carolina. Wow, that's big!

At least 2 million asteroids orbit in an area between Mars and Jupiter. It is called the **asteroid belt**. Many other asteroids share an orbit with Jupiter or Mars.

About seven thousand asteroids come close to Earth's orbit. Worried that one of them might hit our planet? Don't be. Scientists are keeping a close eye on all the near-Earth asteroids.

Q: What did the asteroid say to the meteoroid?

A: "You're a chip off the old block."

Q: Why do some asteroids come so close to Earth?

A: They like the view.

9 Jupiter Is King

Mercury, Venus, Earth, and Mars are all rocky planets. But Jupiter is made mostly of gases. So are Saturn, Neptune, and Uranus. All four outer planets are called **gas giants**.

But Jupiter is the biggest of all. In fact, it's bigger than all the other planets put together.

Jupiter is surrounded by four rings. And it has at least sixty-three moons. That's more than any other planet!

Jupiter's best-known feature is the Great Red Spot. It's the largest storm in the solar system. And it's been raging for at least 180 years.

Jupiter has the shortest days in the solar system. They are just ten hours long. But a year on Jupiter is ten times longer than a year on Earth.

Q: Why is Earth glad to be so far away from Jupiter?

A: Because Jupiter is such a gassy planet.

BEANS! BEANS! THE MUSICAL FRUIT!

Q: Where did Jupiter go on vacation?

A: The galax-sea.

Q: What was the name of Jupiter's big pet dog?

A: Great Red Spot.

Saturn Is Queen

Saturn is the second largest planet in the solar system. And, like Jupiter, it has a whole lot of moons. How many? At least sixty-two!

Saturn is the only planet with rings bright enough to be seen with a low-power telescope. The lovely bands are made of ice, dust, and bits of rock. Some pieces are as small as your pinky fingernail. Others are as large as a house.

Saturn's solid core is a sizzling 21,600°F (12,000°C). That's why the planet releases more heat into space than it gets from the Sun.

Saturn spins so quickly that its days are just a little more than ten hours long. A year on Saturn lasts 10,759 Earth days. That's almost thirty Earth years.

Q: Why did Saturn ask for a necklace on Valentine's Day?

A: Because it already has so many rings.

Q: What did Jupiter say when Saturn asked why Jupiter got the bigger piece of cake?

A: "Because I'm bigger than you."

Q: What does Saturn have in common with an apple?

A: They both have a core.

Unusual Uranus

Uranus doesn't get as much attention as its neighbors. But it's a pretty amazing place. A day on Uranus lasts about seventeen hours. A year is about eighty-four times longer than a year on Earth. Wow!

Say "rings," and most people think of Saturn. But Uranus has more. Nine rings and at least twenty-seven moons circle the blue-green planet.

Say "storms," and most people think of Jupiter. But Uranus has much harder rains. Some storms produce sleet or hail made of diamond. You can't get any harder than that!

Uranus also has the strangest seasons. Because the planet is tipped on its side, each pole has forty-two years of darkness followed by forty-two years of light. Talk about extremes!

Q: Why don't aliens live on Uranus?

A: Because they don't want to wait so long between birthdays.

Q: Why does Uranus have so many friends?

Happy Birthday!

A: Because it's cool.

Q: What did the comet say as it whizzed past Uranus?

A: "How about giving me a ring sometime?"

Nifty Neptune

Neptune is far out—more than 2.7 billion miles (4.4 billion km) from the Sun. The big blue planet takes 165 Earth years to orbit the Sun. But a day on Neptune is just sixteen hours long.

Neptune has plenty of neighbors. Four faint rings and at least thirteen moons circle the gas giant.

What are the icy planet's claims to fame? It has two. It's the farthest planet from the Sun. And it has the strongest winds ever recorded. During a hurricane on Earth, wind gusts max out at 150 miles (240 km) per hour. Think that's fast? Then hold on to your hat! Neptune's whipping winds can reach speeds of 1,200 miles (1,900 km) per hour.

Q: Where do asteroids go to party?

A: Nep-tune. It always has great music.

Q: Why is Neptune so blue?

A: Because it wants to be closer to its Sun.

27

13 Don't Forget the Dwarfs!

Poor Pluto! From 1930 to 2006, scientists thought it was a real, honest-to-goodness planet. But the more they learned about far-out objects, the more they wondered about Pluto.

Today, scientists say Pluto is one of five known dwarf planets. The others are Ceres, Haumea, Makemake, and Eris. Most scientists think there are at least two hundred more dwarfs yet to be discovered. Some say there may be as many as two thousand dwarf planets.

Eris is the largest dwarf planet, and it has one moon. Next comes Pluto, which has three moons. Haumea has two moons. But Makemake and Ceres are on their own.

Ceres is a member of the asteroid belt. All the other dwarf planets orbit beyond Neptune.

Q: What do dwarf planets do every morning?

A: They sing, "Heigh-ho! Heigh-ho! It's off to work we go."

Q: Why didn't the dwarf planet ever tell jokes?

A: Because he was too Ceres-ous.

What's the Kuiper Belt?

What do you think of when someone says "solar system"? The Sun? The Moon? The eight planets? Well then, here's a surprise. Scientists believe that more than 99.9 percent of the solar system lies beyond the orbit of Neptune. That's a lot of space!

The planets are surrounded by a huge area of space called the Kuiper belt. It's home to three of the dwarf planets—Pluto, Haumea, and Makemake. Scientists have also spotted at least 1,300 smaller icy objects there. And that's just the beginning. The belt may contain more than 100,000 objects that are more than 30 miles (50 km) across. Wow!

Q: Which dwarf planet has signs of life?

A: Scientists think there are fleas on Pluto.

Q: What kind of doughnuts do dwarf planets like best?

A: Munchkins.

This is an illustration of a Kuiper belt object.

Q: What does Haumea use to hold up its pants?

A: A Kuiper belt.

A Mess of Moons

When we look up at the night sky, the first thing we might notice is our Moon. It circles Earth once every twenty-seven days.

Many other planets have moons of their own. In fact, at least 168 moons orbit the eight planets. But that's not all. In fact, it's only half the story.

Six moons circle three of the dwarf planets. At least 104 moons orbit asteroids. And we know of 58 moons moving around small objects in the Kuiper belt. That's a lot of moons—336 in all! And scientists think there are many more yet to be discovered.

Q: Why didn't the Moon have ice cream for dessert?

A: It was too full.

Q: Why did the cow jump over the Moon?

A: To get to the other side.

What's the Scatter?

An area called the scattered disk overlaps part of the Kuiper belt. And it stretches far, far out into space. The scattered disk is twice as big as the area occupied by the eight planets plus the Kuiper belt. Now that's pretty big!

What's in the scattered disk? Lots of small icy objects. The biggest one is named Eris. It is a dwarf planet.

Sometimes the icy objects get knocked out of their orbits. Then they become **comets**. Comets race toward the Sun in a new orbit shaped like a cucumber.

When a comet gets close to the Sun, it begins to melt. It gives off gases that glow. The gases form a long tail that can stretch up to 155 million miles (250 million km).

JUPITER

SATURN

Q: What did the Kuiper belt say to the scattered disk?

A: "You're far out!"

Q: What does the Sun do when it's thirsty?

A: It gets out its sun glasses and melts a comet.

Q: What did the Kuiper belt say to the icy object?

A: "You're a knockout!"

PLUTO

NEPTUNE

URANUS

KUIPER BELT

On the Edge

The scattered disk isn't at the edge of the solar system. Not by a long shot. That honor goes to the Oort cloud. Its outer edge is at least ten thousand times farther from the Sun than Neptune.

The Oort cloud is huge. And it may contain as many as 2 trillion icy objects. Yup, that's right, 2 TRILLION. The largest Oort cloud object is called Sedna. It takes 12,050 years to orbit the Sun.

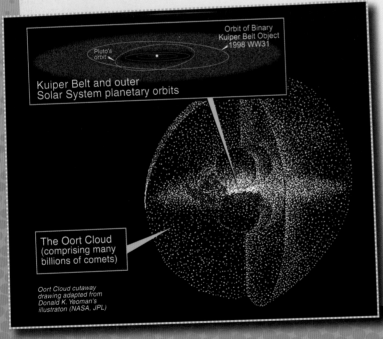

Orbit of Binary
Kuiper Belt Object
1998 WW31

Pluto's
orbit

Kuiper Belt and outer
Solar System planetary orbits

The Oort Cloud
(comprising many
billions of comets)

Oort Cloud cutaway
drawing adapted from
Donald K. Yeoman's
illustraton (NASA, JPL)

Like the icy objects in the scattered disk, objects in the Oort cloud can become comets. Scientists think any comet that takes more than 200 years to orbit the Sun comes from the Oort cloud.

Q: Why did the comet head toward the edge of the solar system?

A: It needed some space.

Q: Why didn't the alien fly into the Oort cloud?

A: He left his umbrella and raincoat at home.

How to Write Your Own Jokes

Writing jokes isn't hard if you keep three helpful hints in mind:

1. Try to think of a joke's punch line, or answer, first. Then work backward to come up with the setup, or question.

2. Keep the setup short and simple. People who listen to your joke will want to try to guess the answer. That's half the fun. But if the question is too long, your listeners won't be able to remember it all. They'll feel frustrated instead of excited.

3. Keep the answer short and simple too. That way it will pack more of a punch.

Popular Expressions

Ever hear someone say: "You're a chip off the old block"? It means you have a lot in common with your mom or dad.

Can you can use this popular expression as the punch line for a joke? You bet!

When asteroids collide, they shatter to form dozens of meteoroids. That means a meteoroid really is a "chip" off an asteroid. So here's a question that works perfectly with your punch line:

Q: What did the asteroid say to the meteoroid?

A: "You're a chip off the old block."

Can you think of another joke that uses a popular expression as a punch line?

Homographs and Homophones

A homograph is a word with two or more different meanings. One example is the word *star*. It can mean "a shining body in the sky" or "a famous person."

You can create a question that seems to use one definition of the word and an answer that uses the other. Here's an example:

Q: Why was the asteroid unhappy?

A: He knew he'd never be a star.

Homophones are two or more words that sound the same, but are spelled differently and have different meanings. For example, the words *meteor* and *meatier* are homophones.

You can create a great joke by mixing homophones. Here's an example:

Q: Why did the asteroid eat a hot dog instead of mac and cheese?

A: Because a hot dog is meteor.

These jokes are fun because your family and friends might be able to guess the answers. And sometimes they'll come up with different answers that are just as good. Then you'll have some brand-new jokes to tell someone else.

You can have lots of fun using homographs and homophones to create jokes that will amuse your friends.

Ha Ha Ha

Similar Sounds, Different Meanings

Changing a few letters can also result in words that sound almost the same, like *lion* and *lying* or *cheetah* and *cheater*. And these word pairs can be the inspiration for some hilarious jokes.

Here's an example:

Q: Why didn't the dwarf planet ever tell jokes?

A: Because he was too Ceres-ous.

This joke works because adding the *–ous* ending to the dwarf planet's name leads to a nonsense word that sound very similar to *serious*.

Can you think of your own space joke that uses similar-sounding words in a funny way?

Rhyme Time

Playing with words to create rhymes can be highly entertaining. It's even better when a rhyme is the heart of a joke. Here's an example:

Q: What do astronauts use to change the radio station when they're on the Moon?

A: A lunar tuner.

Getting Silly

Sometimes the best jokes are ones that are just plain silly or ridiculous. Get ready to laugh out loud—here are some great examples:

Q: How did Mars become the red planet?

A: It stayed out in the Sun too long.

Q: Why don't aliens live on Uranus?

A: Because they don't want to wait so long between birthdays.

Your Jokes in Print

Now it's your turn. See if you can come up with some seriously silly jokes of your own. Then share them with your family and friends.

You can submit your most science-sational jokes to:
mas@melissa-stewart.com
Be sure to include your first name and your age.

The best jokes will be posted on Fridays at:
http://celebratescience.blogspot.com
People all over the world will be able to read and enjoy them. You can send drawings too.Now get to work on some jokes, and don't forget to have a good time!

Words to Know

asteroid—A rocky body that orbits the Sun. An asteroid is larger than a meteoroid but smaller than a planet.

asteroid belt—A region of space between Mars and Jupiter. Many asteroids are found there.

atmosphere—The layer of gases that surrounds a planet or other body in space.

comet—A small ball of rock and ice that orbits the Sun.

core—The innermost layer of Earth and some other space objects.

crater—A hole on the surface of a space body. It forms when a smaller object crashes into a larger one.

crust—The outermost layer of Earth.

day—The time it takes a planet to complete one full spin on its axis.

gas giant—A large planet made primarily of hydrogen, helium, and other gases. Jupiter, Saturn, Uranus, and Neptune are gas giants.

gravity—The force that pulls objects toward the center of a planet or other body in space.

mantle—The central layer of Earth. It contains hot, liquid rock called magma.

meteor—The glowing lights we see in the night sky when a meteoroid is in contact with Earth's atmosphere.

meteorite—A meteoroid that strikes the surface of a planet or other object in space.

meteoroid—A small rocky object in space. Many meteoroids are broken bits of a comet or asteroid.

meteor shower—An event in which we see a large number of meteors coming from the same area of the sky within a short period of time.

moon—A space object that orbits a planet, asteroid, or other larger body that is not a star.

orbit—The path of a body in space as it moves around a larger object with more gravitational pull.

ring—A group of small rocky objects that orbit a planet.

solar system—The Sun and all the objects that orbit it.

year—The amount of time it takes a planet or other space body to orbit the Sun once.

Read More

Books

Carson, Mary Kay. *Exploring the Solar System*. Chicago: Chicago Review Press, 2008.

Simon, Seymour. *Our Solar System*. New York: HarperCollins, 2007.

Wittels, Harriet, and Joan Grelsman. *A First Thesaurus*. New York: Golden Books, 2001.

Young, Sue. *Scholastic Rhyming Dictionary*. New York: Scholastic, 2006.

Internet Addresses

Astronomy for Kids: Our Solar System

<http://www.kidsastronomy.com/solar_system.htm>

Solar System Exploration Kids

<http://solarsystem.nasa.gov/kids/>

Index